J   Duiing, Kaitlyn
BIO
JAMES   LeBron James

In the Spotlight

LeBron James

by Kaitlyn Duling

Bullfrog
Books

Ideas for Parents and Teachers

Bullfrog Books let children practice reading informational text at the earliest reading levels. Repetition, familiar words, and photo labels support early readers.

Before Reading
- Discuss the cover photo. What does it tell them?
- Look at the picture glossary together. Read and discuss the words.

Read the Book
- "Walk" through the book and look at the photos. Let the child ask questions. Point out the photo labels.
- Read the book to the child, or have him or her read independently.

After Reading
- Prompt the child to think more. Ask: What did you know about LeBron James before reading this book? What more would you like to learn about him after reading it?

Bullfrog Books are published by Jump!
5357 Penn Avenue South
Minneapolis, MN 55419
www.jumplibrary.com

Library of Congress Cataloging-in-Publication Data

Names: Duling, Kaitlyn, author.
Title: Lebron James / by Kaitlyn Duling.
Description: Bullfrog Books edition.
Minneapolis, MN : Jump!, Inc., 2018.
Includes index.
Identifiers: LCCN 2018006168 (print)
LCCN 2018003080 (ebook)
ISBN 9781641280426 (ebook)
ISBN 9781641280402 (hardcover : alk. paper)
ISBN 9781641280419 (pbk.)
Subjects: LCSH: James, LeBron—Juvenile literature. | Basketball players—United States Biography—Juvenile literature. | African American basketball players—Biography—Juvenile literature.
Classification: LCC GV884.J36 (print)
LCC GV884.J36 D85 2018 (ebook)
DDC 796.323092 [B]—dc23
LC record available at https://lccn.loc.gov/2018006168

Editor: Jenna Trnka
Designer: Molly Ballanger

Photo Credits: Jason Miller/Getty, cover, 1, 4, 23tl, 24; Rick Scuteri/AP/REX/Shutterstock, 3; Marcio Jose Sanchez/AP/REX/Shutterstock, 5, 23br; Sean Pavone/Shutterstock, 6; Harry How/Getty, 6–7; Vaughn Ridley/Getty, 8; Maddie Meyer/Getty, 9; El Nuevo Herald/Getty, 10–11, 23tr; ESB Professional/Shutterstock, 12; Mike Ehrmann/Getty, 12–13; Angelo Merendino/Getty, 14–15, 23bl; VCG/Getty, 16; Dean Mouhtaropoulos/Getty, 17; Andrew Powell/Getty, 18–19; Marco Secchi/Getty, 20–21; ED BETZ/AP/REX/Shutterstock, 22l; Marcio Jose Sanchez/AP Images, 22r.

Printed in the United States of America at Corporate Graphics in North Mankato, Minnesota.

Table of Contents

LeBron

This is LeBron James.
He is famous. Why?

He plays for the NBA.

He plays for Cleveland.

The team is the Cavaliers.

Cleveland

He dribbles.

He shoots!

LeBron scores points.
He helps win games.
He is an MVP!

He played for Miami.
The team was
the Heat.

Miami

GREE

4

fans

But he came back
to Cleveland.

The fans were happy.

LeBron was back!

Fans love him.

He is kind.

He helps kids.

He gives his time.

He gives money.

DATE 15/10/11

$10,000

...pool FC Foundation

...n Thousand Dollars

Fans love LeBron.
He is a good player.
He is a great
helper, too.

Key Events

February 20, 2005:
LeBron plays in his first NBA All-Star Game.

December 30, 1984:
LeBron Raymone James is born in Akron, Ohio.

June 19, 2016:
LeBron helps Cleveland win the city's first professional sports title in 52 years.

June 26, 2003:
The Cleveland Cavaliers pick LeBron in the NBA draft.

July 10, 2010:
LeBron joins the Miami Heat. Cleveland fans are upset.

May 21, 2017:
LeBron wins the J. Walter Kennedy Citizenship Award. This award honors a player's dedication to community service.

Picture Glossary

famous
Very well-known to many people.

MVP
Most Valuable Player; the award given to the best performing player each season.

fans
People who are very interested in and enthusiastic about something or someone.

NBA
National Basketball Association; the men's professional basketball league in North America.

Index

To Learn More

Learning more is as easy as 1, 2, 3.

1) Go to www.factsurfer.com

2) Enter "LeBronJames" into the search box.

3) Click the "Surf" button to see a list of websites.

With factsurfer.com, finding more information is just a click away.